To
_____

From
_____

Date
_____

Prayer-Letters to Heaven and God's Refreshing Response

Heavenly Mail

Debbie Webb

words of *wisdom* from God

HOWARD
PUBLISHING CO.

Our purpose at Howard Publishing is to:

- *Increase faith* in the hearts of growing Christians
- *Inspire holiness* in the lives of believers
- *Instill hope* in the hearts of struggling people everywhere

Because He's coming again!

Heavenly Mail—Words of Wisdom from God © 2002 by Debbie Webb
All rights reserved. Printed in Mexico
Published by Howard Publishing Co., Inc.
3117 North 7th Street, West Monroe, Louisiana 71291-2227

02 03 04 05 06 07 08 09 10 11   10 9 8 7 6 5 4 3 2

Interior design by Steve Diggs
Edited by Jennifer Stair

1-58229-233-7

For the LORD gives wisdom,

and from his mouth comes

knowledge and understanding.

Proverbs 2:6

Contents

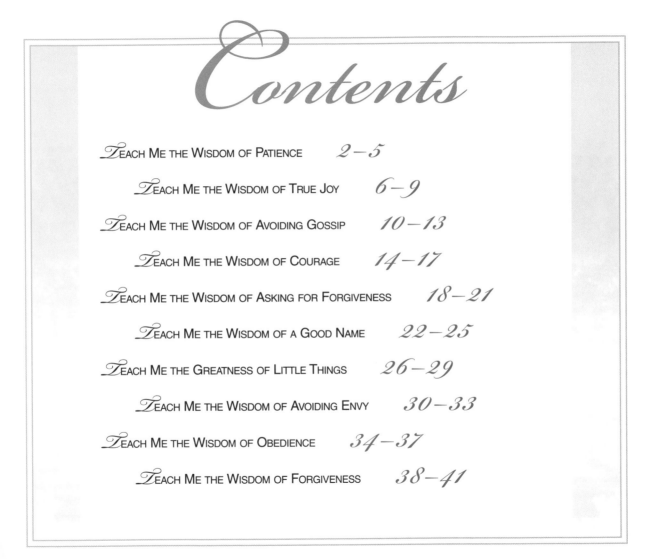

A Word to the Reader

Writing a letter is a special way to express yourself to someone you care for. It allows you to convey your feelings, thoughts, and emotions in a way unlike any other.

And what about receiving mail in return? Who doesn't enjoy the feeling of going to the mailbox, opening the door, and finding that you've got mail? With anticipation, you open the envelope and read the words of a cherished loved one or a faraway friend. Even though the writer is not present, you feel the warmth that the two of you share, and your hearts are united once again. That's what happens when you read *Heavenly Mail: Words of Wisdom from God*.

This unique book is filled with letters between someone like yourself and the very best Friend of all—your heavenly Father. You'll quickly identify with the prayers, written as letters to a loving God, because they convey the needs, emotions, feelings, and struggles that life presents on a regular basis. In heaven's response, you'll read words of wisdom from God based on Scripture, also written as letters, and you'll experience the assuring presence and loving warmth that only heaven can give.

The wisdom that fills these heavenly letters will remain with you, inspire you, and fill you with hope. Let this little book bring you closer to heaven and to words of wisdom that will impact your todays, tomorrows, and the rest of your life.

A LETTER TO *Heaven*

Dear God of Great Patience,

I feel like I'm at the ragged end of a rugged day. It started out badly and kept getting worse until finally, I just blew up.

I woke up tired and temperamental this morning. There wasn't any orange juice for breakfast for the second time this week. How difficult can it be to keep orange juice in plentiful supply?

I stopped by the drugstore to pick up a prescription, and already late for work, I backed into a car behind me, crushing my taillight. I dented the bumper on the other car, and the driver was very angry. It took forty-five minutes to complete the police report.

When I got to my desk, I realized that I had missed the first thirty minutes of an early meeting that my boss had scheduled yesterday. The discussion concerning my department was completed before I ever entered the room.

And finally, when I picked the kids up from the baby-sitter this evening, my son had been bitten by another child and had a bruise on his arm.

I've told You all of this so that You'll understand why I yelled at my spouse when I found out that supper was going to be late.

Lord, I consider myself a patient person, but everyone has limits, and I felt I had reached mine. I'm truly sorry that I lost my cool, and I know that it was wrong. How can I keep from losing my temper under circumstances like these? I really want to learn patience, Lord.

Your Hot-Tempered Child

2

A LETTER FROM *Heaven*

Dear Hot-Tempered Child,

Everyone has days when everything seems to go wrong. It makes you wish you could crawl back into bed and stay there—safe from the difficulties that life imposes. Sometimes you can't escape the feeling that everyone would be better off if you just stayed out of circulation for a day.

Let me encourage you to consider this: Patience is really a matter of perspective. When things start piling up and you begin to feel overwhelmed by the pressures of life, just remember that you are not alone. Many times your impatience is a result of feeling as if you are on your own, as if no one is there for you. A panic swells within your spirit and washes over your heart. You fly off the handle because you don't feel adequately supported.

I assure you, My child, that I am with you. If you will turn to Me, I will generously supply all that you need. Whether you need wisdom, insight, patience, support, strength, or encouragement, I will be there for you.

When you feel anger in times of stress, find a time and a quiet place where we can talk. I know you are busy and hurried, but that is part of the problem. You need to slow down. Pour out your heart and your anxiety into my lap of love, and I can make a difference.

Remember, everyone has a bad day once in a while. Just make sure that your bad days are not outnumbering your good days.

Your Patient Father

God's Word OF WISDOM

PROVERBS 19:19
A hot-tempered man must pay the penalty; if you rescue him, you will have to do it again.

EPHESIANS 4:1–3
As a prisoner for the Lord, then, I urge you to live a life worthy of the calling you have received. Be completely humble and gentle; be patient, bearing with one another in love. Make every effort to keep the unity of the Spirit through the bond of peace.

PROVERBS 14:29
A patient man has great understanding, but a quick-tempered man displays folly.

EPHESIANS 4:29–32
Do not let any unwholesome talk come out of your mouths, but only what is helpful for building others up according to their needs, that it may benefit those who listen. And do not grieve the Holy Spirit of God, with whom you were sealed for the day of redemption. Get rid of all bitterness, rage and anger, brawling and slander, along with every form of malice. Be kind and compassionate to one another, forgiving each other, just as in Christ God forgave you.

PROVERBS 22:24–25
Do not make friends with a hot-tempered man, do not associate with one easily angered, or you may learn his ways and get yourself ensnared.

JAMES 1:19–20
My dear brothers, take note of this: Everyone should be quick to listen, slow to speak and slow to become angry, for man's anger does not bring about the righteous life that God desires.

EPHESIANS 4:26–27
"In your anger do not sin": Do not let the sun go down while you are still angry, and do not give the devil a foothold.

2 TIMOTHY 2:22–26
Flee the evil desires of youth, and pursue righteousness, faith, love and peace, along with those who call on the Lord out of a pure heart. Don't have anything to do with foolish and stupid arguments, because you know they produce quarrels. And the Lord's servant must not quarrel; instead, he must be kind to everyone, able to teach, not resentful. Those who oppose him he must gently instruct, in the hope that God will grant them repentance leading them to a knowledge of the truth, and that they will come to their senses and escape from the trap of the devil, who has taken them captive to do his will.

A LETTER TO *Heaven*

Dear God of Joy,

Lord, I want to reflect Your joy to the world, but I just haven't felt very joyful lately. Someone once told me that at age five we laugh approximately five hundred times a day but that by the time we are forty, we laugh fewer than five times a day. What is it about life, Lord, that robs us of our joy?

I know that joy, unlike happiness, doesn't depend on our circumstances. I have seen people rejoice at the most unexpected times, like at the funeral of a loved one or in the aftermath of a house fire. And I have seen others distraught over the least little misfortune, like breaking a fingernail or getting a flat tire. I have observed mothers scowling at their children for little acts of irritation in the grocery store. Then, on the other hand, I have watched fathers smiling through tears of heartache in hospital corridors.

One thing I have noticed is that people who reflect true joy in their hearts are greatly loved. They seem to have great influence in the lives of others. People run to them for counsel, comfort, and companionship. They seem to derive great benefit from the simplest pleasures in life. They seem to have great peace and contentment. They seem to have insight into things that others can't see.

I want to be like them, Lord. What is the source of true joy? How can I experience real joy in this difficult world?

Your Curious Child

A LETTER FROM *Heaven*

Dear Curious Child,

You are right about laughter diminishing as life wears on. It causes Me sorrow to see joy dissipating in the hearts of My children as they grow older.

Naturally, the innocence of childhood shields you from many hard truths about life. As you age, you are forced to deal with more difficult issues that may rob you of your joy.

True joy comes from having a deeply rooted faith in Me and a deeply ingrained hope in My promises. When you find that the foundation of your life rests upon the rock of eternal truth, you aren't as invested in temporary circumstances or as distressed by inconveniences. In fact, death itself casts a dimmer shadow upon the hearts of those whose light is the Lord. It is merely a passage through which eternal life is gained.

Joy is a condition of the heart; it is an attitude about your earthly existence based upon a heavenly perspective. Joy does not anchor itself in the shifting sands of earthly events. It is planted solidly in grace and the promises of heaven's abundance.

Joy is elusive only to those who are unwilling to look beyond their own desires, their own needs, and their own circumstances for fulfillment.

You will be able to maintain true joy only by seeking it in relationship with Me and extending it in relationship to others. You will find its definition in valuing what I value. And you will find that joy fills the lives and heals the hearts of all who live for Jesus.

Your God of Joy

God's Word OF WISDOM

PROVERBS 15:13
A happy heart makes the face cheerful, but
heartache crushes the spirit.

PHILIPPIANS 4:4–5
Rejoice in the Lord always. I will say it
again: Rejoice! Let your gentleness be
evident to all. The Lord is near.

JAMES 1:2–5
Consider it pure joy, my brothers,
whenever you face trials of many
kinds, because you know that the
testing of your faith develops
perseverance. Perseverance must
finish its work so that you may be
mature and complete, not lacking
anything. If any of you lacks
wisdom, he should ask God, who
gives generously to all without
finding fault, and it will be given
to him.

LUKE 2:8–11
There were shepherds living out in the fields nearby, keeping
watch over their flocks at night. An angel of the Lord
appeared to them, and the glory of the Lord shone around
them, and they were terrified. But the angel said to them, "Do
not be afraid. I bring you good news of great joy that will be
for all the people. Today in the town of David a Savior has
been born to you; he is Christ the Lord."

PROVERBS 12:25
An anxious heart weighs a man down,
but a kind word cheers him up.

NEHEMIAH 8:10
Do not grieve, for the joy of the LORD is
your strength.

JOHN 16:20, 22–24
I tell you the truth, you will weep and mourn while
the world rejoices. You will grieve, but your grief
will turn to joy. Now is your time of grief, but I will
see you again and you will rejoice, and no one will
take away your joy. In that day you will no longer
ask me anything. I tell you the truth, my Father will
give you whatever you ask in my name. Until now
you have not asked for anything in my name. Ask
and you will receive, and your joy will be complete.

PROVERBS 17:22
A cheerful heart is good
medicine, but a crushed
spirit dries up the bones.

A  Letter to *Heaven*

Dear Faithful Father,

I just said something I know I shouldn't have, and I feel awful. I didn't mean to gossip; in fact, I didn't even see the temptation coming until I heard the words coming out of my mouth. But now the damage has been done, and I can't take it back.

That happens to me frequently, Lord. I don't set out to harm people, but I start talking, and before I realize what is happening, I've said something I shouldn't.

Father, how can I keep from falling into the gossip trap over and over again? I'm ashamed of myself when I hurt someone's reputation with my words. Besides, I know I'm hurting my own reputation as well. Who would trust a person who tells everything she knows?

In my heart, I want to be different. I want to be like others who choose their words more carefully. How do they do that, Father? Teach me what I need to know to make better choices about these matters. What should determine what I say and what I don't say?

Your Growing Child

A LETTER FROM *Heaven*

Dear Growing Child,

You are learning that it is not wise for you to say everything you know or everything that enters into your heart. Your heart is not always pure, and your head is not always clear. The measure by which you can determine what you should and should not say is known as discretion, and it is essential for living effectively among others.

There are two sides of discretion. The first is selection. It is so important that you learn the value of sorting through the things you know and the feelings you have before you speak. Select carefully only those things that will be uplifting and beneficial—not only to the hearer, but also to everyone else who might be affected by your words, directly or indirectly. You will find that choosing words with the motive of blessing others will always serve you well.

The other side of discretion is restraint. You will always know more and feel more than you should say aloud. People sometimes make the mistake of thinking that the truth of a matter is valid reason for telling it or that the presence of an emotion is justifiable reason for expressing it. Not so! The thing may be true but wrong to say. Your feelings may be real but wrong to express. Restraint involves the self-discipline to exercise the selection you made for all the right reasons.

Be sure, My child, that you will be blessed by learning discretion.

Your Faithful Father

God's Word OF WISDOM

PROVERBS 11:9
With his mouth the godless destroys his neighbor, but through knowledge the righteous escape.

PROVERBS 20:19
A gossip betrays a confidence; so avoid a man who talks too much.

PROVERBS 11:13
A gossip betrays a confidence, but a trustworthy man keeps a secret.

PHILIPPIANS 4:8
Finally, brothers, whatever is true, whatever is noble, whatever is right, whatever is pure, whatever is lovely, whatever is admirable—if anything is excellent or praiseworthy—think about such things.

PROVERBS 17:9
He who covers over an offense promotes love, but whoever repeats the matter separates close friends.

MATTHEW 7:12

So in everything, do to others what you would have them do to you, for this sums up the Law and the Prophets.

PROVERBS 10:13–14

Wisdom is found on the lips of the discerning, but a rod is for the back of him who lacks judgment. Wise men store up knowledge, but the mouth of a fool invites ruin.

PROVERBS 10:18–19

He who conceals his hatred has lying lips, and whoever spreads slander is a fool. When words are many, sin is not absent, but he who holds his tongue is wise.

PROVERBS 11:12

A man who lacks judgment derides his neighbor, but a man of understanding holds his tongue.

A LETTER TO *Heaven*

Dear Courageous Father,

There is a terrible fear stalking my heart. It plagues me constantly during my waking hours and even in my dreams at night. It suffocates my creativity and sabotages my ability to reason. I try to resist its haunting voice, but I cannot win.

I have finally identified this fear: I am afraid of failing.

Lord, I try so hard to overcome this fear by reasoning with it. I tell myself that I have every reason to be confident. I am a capable person with a good mind. I am diligent and thorough in everything I do. I have strong morals, and I am fair and considerate of others. But in spite of all of that, I am still afraid of failure.

What if I don't succeed at my job? What if I fail my friends or family? How could I possibly be the kind of person that You want me to be?

Father, increase my faith! Speak the words to me that will give my heart courage and chase away my fear.

Your Fearful Child

A LETTER FROM *Heaven*

Dear Fearful Child,

Your fear of failure is not uncommon. Most people deal with it intermittently, wrestling to resolve whether they have done all within their power to ensure their own success. Your obsession with it, however, is distracting you from your productivity and interfering with your potential.

Fear is a condition of a heart that is too self-reliant. You have accepted more than your share of the responsibility to succeed in your endeavors. You have somehow determined that you are all you have to depend upon, when in reality you have all the reinforcements of heaven in place.

Your fear is really a relational dilemma. Instead of spending your energies trying to reason harder and perform better, you really need more of Me in your heart, more time in My Word, more time spent in prayer. You need to concentrate your thoughts on Who is really in control. And since it isn't you, you can relax a bit, breathe a little easier, and rest awhile. I have everything in hand. In fact, you can insist upon a blessing from a Father who loves you more than you can ever comprehend, knowing that I will lavish you with My great love in response to your asking in faith.

In short, the only way to deal with your fears is to focus not on what you fear but on Me. Discovering who I am will put all that you fear into perfect perspective. I am greater than your greatest fear.

Your Courageous Father

God's Word OF WISDOM

2 KINGS 6:16
"Don't be afraid," the prophet answered. "Those who are with us are more than those who are with them."

2 TIMOTHY 1:7
God did not give us a spirit of timidity, but a spirit of power, of love and of self-discipline.

PSALM 20:1–2, 4
May the LORD answer you when you are in distress; may the name of the God of Jacob protect you. May he send you help from the sanctuary and grant you support from Zion. May he give you the desire of your heart and make all your plans succeed.

ROMANS 8:35, 37–39
Who shall separate us from the love of Christ? Shall trouble or hardship or persecution or famine or nakedness or danger or sword? No, in all these things we are more than conquerors through him who loved us. For I am convinced that neither death nor life, neither angels nor demons, neither the present nor the future, nor any powers, neither height nor depth, nor anything else in all creation, will be able to separate us from the love of God that is in Christ Jesus our Lord.

PSALM 16:7–8
I will praise the LORD, who counsels me; even at night my heart instructs me. I have set the LORD always before me. Because he is at my right hand, I will not be shaken.

JOSHUA 23:3
You yourselves have seen everything the LORD your God has done to all these nations for your sake; it was the LORD your God who fought for you.

16

2 CHRONICLES 32:7–8

Be strong and courageous. Do not be afraid or discouraged...,for there is a greater power with us than with him. With him is only the arm of flesh, but with us is the LORD our God to help us and to fight our battles.

PSALM 16:1–2

Keep me safe, O God, for in you I take refuge. I said to the LORD, "You are my Lord; apart from you I have no good thing."

EXODUS 14:13–14

Moses answered the people, "Do not be afraid. Stand firm and you will see the deliverance the LORD will bring you today.... The LORD will fight for you; you need only to be still."

PSALM 18:1–3, 6

I love you, O LORD, my strength. The LORD is my rock, my fortress and my deliverer; my God is my rock, in whom I take refuge. He is my shield and the horn of my salvation, my stronghold. I call to the LORD, who is worthy of praise, and I am saved from my enemies. In my distress I called to the LORD; I cried to my God for help. From his temple he heard my voice; my cry came before him, into his ears.

ROMANS 8:31

What, then, shall we say in response to this? If God is for us, who can be against us?

A LETTER TO *Heaven*

Dear Faithful Father,

Several days ago I did something to a friend that I shouldn't have done. I knew it was wrong when I did it, but I justified my actions by thinking only of myself. It hurt my friend deeply, and I have allowed days to go by without addressing it. Now the wound has festered in her heart, and she is more deeply pained than when the wrong occurred because I was unwilling to ask forgiveness while it was fresh.

Why is it so hard to say, "I'm sorry"? Is it because the implications are so humbling? After all, "I'm sorry" also means "I was wrong, I am insensitive, and I am selfish." Who likes to admit to being wrong, much less insensitive and selfish?

Well, by putting off my apology I've added to that list of admissions: "I am prideful." It is getting harder to ask for her forgiveness because the pain seems to be growing with each moment that passes between us. We can't communicate the way we always have because there is so much tension between us. We can't laugh together because our joy has been strained. We can't even be kind to one another because I have violated her trust by my actions and my failure to ask forgiveness.

Father, help me break through the walls of my heart and humble myself in order to start the healing of this relationship.

Your Prideful Child

A LETTER FROM *Heaven*

Dear Child in Need of Forgiveness,

It would be wonderful if your heart were so pure that you never hurt others. But you are human, and humans hurt one another. It would be almost as wonderful if, when you do hurt others, you would immediately reach to resolve the dilemma with an attitude of humility and a spirit of repentance. But, again, you are human, and humans rarely do that. It is a good thing that you have come to grips with the fact that you've been stubborn and willful. You are ready to admit your fault, say you are sorry, and salvage the damage that you've done.

Better late than never. But it will be much more difficult now than if you had rushed to make it right immediately.

The one thing that I hope you'll learn, having suffered this heartache by refusing to apologize, is to seek forgiveness as a first recourse rather than a last. There is no point in going through this over and over again when there is nothing to be gained.

Are you aware that your willingness to ask forgiveness immediately would increase trust in the relationship? The wrong done isn't nearly as significant as the desire to make it right again. Those who love you can tolerate your inadequacies but not your insensitivity to their heartache.

Get up off your knees right now and go get right with the one you've hurt. Then we'll continue our conversation.

Your Father Who Forgives You

God's Word OF WISDOM

JAMES 4:6
He gives us more grace. That is why the Scripture says: "God opposes the proud but gives grace to the humble."

JAMES 4:10
Humble yourselves before the Lord, and he will lift you up.

PROVERBS 28:13–14
He who conceals his sins does not prosper, but whoever confesses and renounces them finds mercy. Blessed is the man who always fears the LORD, but he who hardens his heart falls into trouble.

HEBREWS 12:14–15
Make every effort to live in peace with all men and to be holy; without holiness no one will see the Lord. See to it that no one misses the grace of God and that no bitter root grows up to cause trouble and defile many.

JAMES 5:16
Confess your sins to each other and pray for each other so
that you may be healed. The prayer of a righteous man is
powerful and effective.

PROVERBS 17:14
Starting a quarrel is like breaching a dam; so
drop the matter before a dispute breaks out.

MATTHEW 5:23–24
If you are offering your gift at the altar and
there remember that your brother has
something against you, leave your gift
there in front of the altar. First go and be
reconciled to your brother; then come and
offer your gift.

PROVERBS 29:23
A man's pride brings him low, but a
man of lowly spirit gains honor.

A LETTER TO *Heaven*

Dear Heavenly Father,

When my earthly father died, someone said to me, "I guess it is up to you to carry on your father's good name." That statement really got me thinking: What kind of name am I making for myself? I know that a name isn't intrinsically good or bad, so how can I earn the reputation of a *good* name?

I suppose I could give enormous amounts of money to an institution of learning or medicine, and that might give me a good name. I've seen plaques dedicated to those who donate generously to such noble causes. But then, one of the best men I know gave an unbelievable sum of money *anonymously* to fund a private university specializing in missions so that the administration could *not* pay tribute to his name. He seems to think that *not* being known gives him a good name. That confuses the issue for me.

Jesus had a good name according to the common people of His day, yet the religious authorities despised and cursed His name.

How do I go about carrying on my father's good name? How do I determine what constitutes having a good name in the face of society's values? How will I know when my motive is strictly to have a good name rather than to make a name for myself?

Your Confused Child

A LETTER FROM *Heaven*

Dear Confused Child,

It is in living a life of integrity that you derive the *goodness* of your name. It is in blessing others for the sake of building them up that you find your definition. It is in fulfilling your eternal purpose here on earth that you come to attain our true identity.

You are participating in one of the oldest struggles of mankind. Men, from the beginning of time, have wrestled with making a name for themselves as opposed to having a good name.

The true test of having a good name is in the reflection of My character within your identity. Is the name of the Blessed One written all over your good works? Are your motives rooted in glorifying the name of the Almighty or in glorifying yourself? Do you do what you do in order to call attention to yourself or in order to bless others?

Having a good name cannot happen to the passively unconcerned or the disengaged spectators of life who just live for their own pleasures. Nor can it happen to those who simply have the means to publicize themselves with impressive funds or connections.

Having a good name can only come to those who forget themselves long enough and completely enough to lavish selfless love upon others. Speaking kind words in a time of need, lifting a burden too heavy for one to bear alone, relieving the sorrows of grief or shame with companionship and mercy—those are the deeds that establish a good name. Any act that is worthy of My name will ensure you a *good* name.

The Father from Whom You Derived Your Name

God's Word OF WISDOM

PROVERBS 22:1
A good name is more desirable
than great riches.

1 JOHN 3:1
How great is the love the Father has lavished
on us, that we should be called children of
God! And that is what we are!

JOHN 17:11
Holy Father, protect them by the power of
your name—the name you gave me—so that
they may be one as we are one.

PROVERBS 19:1
Better a poor man whose
walk is blameless than a fool
whose lips are perverse.

PROVERBS 25:27
It is not good to eat too much honey,
nor is it honorable to seek one's own
honor.

PROVERBS 27:19
As water reflects a face, so a man's
heart reflects the man.

ECCLESIASTES 7:1
A good name is better than fine perfume.

PROVERBS 10:7
The memory of the righteous will
be a blessing, but the name of the
wicked will rot.

PROVERBS 28:6
Better a poor man whose walk is
blameless than a rich man whose
ways are perverse.

A *L*ETTER TO *Heaven*

Dear God of Great Humility,

Lord, I know You want me to be humble, but I have to tell You—it's not easy. This morning I saw a coworker kicking a can away from the doorway of our building. I challenged her to help keep the premises clean, but she just said, "What do you think I am, a janitor?" Then, yesterday I saw the president of our company picking up trash in the foyer. He doesn't have to do that, but he's a man of deep character, so he couldn't do otherwise.

When I thought about those two people and their different reactions, I had to search my own heart, and I didn't like what I saw. I realized that I'm more like my coworker than my president. When someone asks me to do a noble deed, like speaking to a group of people for a special event, I rise to the occasion like a champion. But when I'm asked to do a menial task, like baby-sitting my brother's children, I come up with a dozen excuses.

The fact is: I don't like tending to tedious matters, Lord. They seem beneath me and make me feel unimportant. I'm embarrassed to admit it, but I like the "loftier" assignments that get more public recognition.

I don't want to be this way. I know that avoiding little acts of service deprives me of greatness in Your eyes. Lord, teach me that there is greatness in little things.

Your Struggling Servant

A *Letter* FROM *Heaven*

Dear Struggling Servant,

Humility is the most difficult quality to maintain within the human heart. There is something within you that craves to be first, to be best, to be noticed, and to be exalted. Anything less, anything common, seems to be beneath your opinion of yourself. However, your opinion of yourself and heaven's opinion of you may be different. You may think too highly of yourself in heaven's estimation.

How can you overcome your pride? You will master it only by the ruthless diligence of self-denial and the rigorous discipline of self-forgetfulness.

When called upon either directly or circumstantially to render a small service or tedious task, rush in upon your heart with relentless self-evaluation. Ask yourself these questions and demand an honest answer: Is this something Jesus would have done? Am I hesitating because it will not benefit me directly? Am I unwilling because someone else will get the credit?

If you find that your pride is being dealt a mortal blow by the demeaning nature of the task, hurry to do it! It is precisely what you need. Out of the ruins of your pride will arise the purified heart of a genuine servant.

Train yourself to find your deepest joy in tending to the things that others are unwilling to do. You will find that self-respect grows as self-centeredness diminishes.

Your God of Great Humility

God's Word OF WISDOM

COLOSSIANS 3:17
Whatever you do,
whether in word or
deed, do it all in the
name of the Lord
Jesus, giving thanks
to God the Father
through him.

MATTHEW 16:24–25
Then Jesus said to his disciples, "If anyone would come after me,
he must deny himself and take up his cross and follow me. For
whoever wants to save his life will lose it, but whoever loses his
life for me will find it."

PROVERBS 25:12
Like an earring of gold or an ornament
of fine gold is a wise man's rebuke to a
listening ear.

EPHESIANS 6:7–8
Serve wholeheartedly, as if you were serving the
Lord, not men, because you know that the Lord will
reward everyone for whatever good he does, whether
he is slave or free.

PROVERBS 27:2
Let another praise you, and not
your own mouth; someone else,
and not your own lips.

PROVERBS 25:6–7
Do not exalt yourself in the king's presence, and do not claim a place among great men; it is better for him to say to you, "Come up here," than for him to humiliate you before a nobleman.

ROMANS 12:16
Live in harmony with one another. Do not be proud, but be willing to associate with people of low position. Do not be conceited.

COLOSSIANS 3:23–24
Whatever you do, work at it with all your heart, as working for the Lord, not for men, since you know that you will receive an inheritance from the Lord as a reward. It is the Lord Christ you are serving.

JOHN 13:14–15
Now that I, your Lord and Teacher, have washed your feet, you also should wash one another's feet. I have set you an example that you should do as I have done for you.

A LETTER TO *Heaven*

Dear Father of Generous Love,

The insidious enemy of envy has crept into my heart. I don't know when it started, but lately it seems to have taken over. Lord, my envy of others is ugly and shameful, yet I have nurtured it and coddled it as though it were the most precious thing in my life.

How has something this dreadful grown to such overwhelming proportions that I am now a prisoner of my own sinful heart? It eats at me, Father, in dark moments of quiet reflection upon the good in other people's lives. At times I am so consumed with envy that I cannot hide it when someone else is applauded or when someone else experiences success.

When there is occasion to rejoice with a friend over a great accomplishment, I see the with jealousy. And I am so ashamed of what is really going on in my heart that I act my way through it only to keep myself in a better light.

I want to have a gracious and generous heart toward others, Lord. I want to be able to genuinely rejoice over the good things in the lives of people I love even when things aren't going well with me.

Help me, Father, to overcome the enemy of envy.

Your Jealous Child

A LETTER FROM *Heaven*

Dear Jealous Child,

The joy you experience in life is like the flow of water in a river. When a river runs its course without receiving the waters of any other tributary, it dwindles along its way, diminishing at every turn and weakening in its current until finally its last trickle is absorbed into the soil, and the river reaches its end.

But when a river runs its course receiving water along the way from streams on both sides, from springs beneath, and from melted snow upon the mountains rushing down in waterfalls, it increases and grows stronger until it pours itself into the ocean with reckless abandon.

If you derive joy only from your own little rivulet of success and abundance, you will eventually dwindle, diminish, and dry up in despair. But if you receive the joys of others as contributions to your own, you will grow and swell and become a source of life and strength for many, gaining momentum toward the end of life as you rush into the eternal ocean of My embrace.

The only way to extract this dreadful enemy of the soul is to cultivate a lavish habit of love. To love generously by getting involved in the joys of others is to deprive envy of its very breath. By getting outside yourself and participating in the successes of others, you will smother the jealous fiend and liberate your heart to live again—abundantly.

My child, take this wisdom to heart and be set free!

Your Father of Gracious Love

God's Word OF WISDOM

1 Peter 2:1
Rid yourselves of all malice and all deceit, hypocrisy, envy, and slander of every kind.

Proverbs 27:4
Anger is cruel and fury overwhelming, but who can stand before jealousy?

2 Corinthians 12:20
I fear that there may be quarreling, jealousy, outbursts of anger, factions, slander, gossip, arrogance and disorder.

Proverbs 14:30
A heart at peace gives life to the body, but envy rots the bones.

Proverbs 11:2–3
When pride comes, then comes disgrace, but with humility comes wisdom. The integrity of the upright guides them, but the unfaithful are destroyed by their duplicity.

PROVERBS 11:6
The righteousness of the upright delivers them, but the unfaithful are trapped by evil desires.

PROVERBS 15:17
Better a meal of vegetables where there is love than a fattened calf with hatred.

PROVERBS 24:1
Do not envy wicked men, do not desire their company.

JAMES 3:13–16
Who is wise and understanding among you? Let him show it by his good life, by deeds done in the humility that comes from wisdom. But if you harbor bitter envy and selfish ambition in your hearts, do not boast about it or deny the truth. Such "wisdom" does not come down from heaven but is earthly, unspiritual, of the devil. For where you have envy and selfish ambition, there you find disorder and every evil practice.

PROVERBS 23:17
Do not let your heart envy sinners, but always be zealous for the fear of the LORD.

A LETTER TO *Heaven*

Dear Heavenly Father,

I feel so victorious! Today I made the difficult choice to stand alone in my convictions while my friends went down a different path. It was very hard in the moment of decision. I wavered a little when they expressed disappointment at my refusal to go along, but my determination to see it through won out, and I overcame in the strength of Your grace.

It feels so good, Lord, having done the right thing. My heart feels joyful, my head is clear, my spirits are light, and I feel somehow closer to You than I have ever felt. I never knew obedience could be so thrilling—so rewarding! Lord, I hope I can remember this wonderful sensation the next time I'm faced with temptation. I hope it will serve to motivate me to live a life of obedience.

What is most surprising of all, Father, is that I feel somehow liberated and energized. Why had I always thought that obedience would be so confining, so restrictive? Why did I have the impression that obedience would mean living with less, when instead my heart is overflowing with joy, peace, courage, and faith?

Lord, help me to grasp the glory of this experience. Help me to hang on hard to Your hand through the next trial I face. And help me to encourage other strugglers I know to join me in the victory.

Your Victorious Child

A *Letter* from *Heaven*

Dear Obedient Child,

I am rejoicing over you! The halls of heaven reverberated with cheers, applause, and shouts of victory when you held your ground against the enemy. Along with Jesus, the saints who walk these gilded streets were praying fervently for your triumph. And We won! We *all* won!

I am thrilled that you have overcome and pleased that you are full of joy.

But be ready, My child, for the battle has just begun. Though the enemy has retreated in defeat, he has not surrendered. He will regroup, rally his troops, and redouble his efforts. You are on the alert now and looking forward to another day of victory. But he is shrewd and may set an ambush, attacking you from behind, where you are vulnerable, unguarded, and unprotected.

Let your joy in Me be your strength for the next encounter. If he strikes, do not shrink back, but march into the battle with your spiritual armor intact. Let My words be the helmet that shields your thinking and keeps you from confusion. Let My righteousness be worn over your heart to keep you from doubting yourself. Let your faith in Me be your shield to deflect his attempts on your confidence so that you can experience yet another victory. In other words, stay close to Me. Pray hard and pray often.

And never fear; I will always be right beside you to protect you.

Your Father Who Rejoices over You

God's Word OF WISDOM

ZEPHANIAH 3:17

The LORD your God is with you, he is mighty to save. He will take great delight in you, he will quiet you with his love, he will rejoice over you with singing.

DEUTERONOMY 5:32–33

Be careful to do what the LORD your God has commanded you; do not turn aside to the right or to the left. Walk in all the way that the LORD your God has commanded you, so that you may live and prosper and prolong your days in the land that you will possess.

JOHN 15:9–11

As the Father has loved me, so have I loved you. Now remain in my love. If you obey my commands, you will remain in my love, just as I have obeyed my Father's commands and remain in his love. I have told you this so that my joy may be in you and that your joy may be complete.

DEUTERONOMY 6:3–7

Hear, O Israel, and be careful to obey so that it may go well with you and that you may increase greatly in a land flowing with milk and honey, just as the LORD, the God of your fathers, promised you. Hear, O Israel: The LORD our God, the LORD is one. Love the LORD your God with all your heart and with all your soul and with all your strength. These commandments that I give you today are to be upon your hearts. Impress them on your children.

36

PSALM 143:10
Teach me to do your will, for you are my God; may your good Spirit lead me on level ground.

TITUS 3:1–2
Remind the people to be subject to rulers and authorities, to be obedient, to be ready to do whatever is good, to slander no one, to be peaceable and considerate, and to show true humility toward all men.

TITUS 2:11–13
For the grace of God that brings salvation has appeared to all men. It teaches us to say "No" to ungodliness and worldly passions, and to live self-controlled, upright and godly lives in this present age, while we wait for the blessed hope—the glorious appearing of our great God and Savior, Jesus Christ.

1 PETER 1:13–16
Prepare your minds for action; be self-controlled; set your hope fully on the grace to be given you when Jesus Christ is revealed. As obedient children, do not conform to evil desires you had when you lived in ignorance. But just as he who called you is holy, so be holy in all you do; for it is written: "Be holy, because I am holy."

A LETTER TO *Heaven*

Dear Forgiving Father,

I am overcome with sorrow. A great rift has occurred in a relationship that I have cherished for so long. I am deeply hurt—crushed under a burden of loss. I cannot imagine ever being able to trust again.

Father, what should we do when someone we love so completely hurts us so desperately? How can this kind of heartache ever heal? I have been devastated by this person's insensitivity, lack of loyalty, and indignant behavior.

I know, Lord, that we all make mistakes in judgment when dealing with people. And I know that we need to be merciful and forgiving when we are wronged, but aren't there limits to what we are expected to endure? I don't recall that I've ever hurt anyone as badly as this person has hurt me. I don't even want to continue in the relationship at this time. I'm not sure that I can ever feel "safe" again.

Lord, I know that You know all things. I believe that You understand my anguish. I trust that You feel my pain. Please counsel me with wisdom from above.

Your Brokenhearted Child

A LETTER FROM *Heaven*

Dear Brokenhearted Child,

I understand your heartache, and I feel your pain. I know the anguish assaulting your heart because someone you love has hurt you deeply.

There is something so defining about experiencing this kind of sorrow. You come to grips with how vulnerable you are when you love. You face the fragile nature of your human heart, and you have decisions to make about whether you'll risk loving again.

Do you remember the first words Jesus spoke when He was crucified? "Father, forgive them; for they do not know what they are doing."

Are you aware that when people sin against you, these words usually apply? People do not realize the extent of their actions. They do not know how wrong they are, they are not aware of how much they are hurting you, nor are they cognizant of how sorry they will be when the dust has settled and the damage is assessed. They are usually acting on sinful impulses and selfish ambition that causes them to rationalize destructive behavior. But when right thinking is restored, their sensitivity will come with it. And too late, they will know.

Understanding this, should you risk loving again? Should you forgive?

My word to you is this: It is worth the risk to love again. Forgive them, not because they deserve it, but because they need it.

And by the way, you will need it too. It's just a matter of time.

Your Forgiving Father

God's Word OF WISDOM

LUKE 23:33–34

When they came to the place called the Skull, there they crucified him, along with the criminals—one on his right, the other on his left. Jesus said, "Father, forgive them, for they do not know what they are doing."

MATTHEW 18:21–22

Then Peter came to Jesus and asked, "Lord, how many times shall I forgive my brother when he sins against me? Up to seven times?" Jesus answered, "I tell you, not seven times, but seventy-seven times."

MATTHEW 6:14–15

If you forgive men when they sin against you, your heavenly Father will also forgive you. But if you do not forgive men their sins, your Father will not forgive your sins.

ISAIAH 53:4–6

Surely he took up our infirmities and carried our sorrows, yet we considered him stricken by God, smitten by him, and afflicted. But he was pierced for our transgressions, he was crushed for our iniquities; the punishment that brought us peace was upon him, and by his wounds we are healed. We all, like sheep, have gone astray, each of us has turned to his own way; and the LORD has laid on him the iniquity of us all.

COLOSSIANS 3:12–15

As God's chosen people, holy and dearly loved, clothe yourselves with compassion, kindness, humility, gentleness and patience. Bear with each other and forgive whatever grievances you may have against one another. Forgive as the Lord forgave you. And over all these virtues put on love, which binds them all together in perfect unity. Let the peace of Christ rule in your hearts, since as members of one body you were called to peace. And be thankful.

ACTS 7:59–60

While they were stoning him, Stephen prayed, "Lord Jesus, receive my spirit." Then he fell on his knees and cried out, "Lord, do not hold this sin against them." When he had said this, he fell asleep.

PROVERBS 19:11

A man's wisdom gives him patience; it is to his glory to overlook an offense.

LAMENTATIONS 3:19–24

I remember my affliction and my wandering, the bitterness and the gall. I well remember them, and my soul is downcast within me. Yet this I call to mind and therefore I have hope: Because of the LORD's great love we are not consumed, for his compassions never fail. They are new every morning; great is your faithfulness. I say to myself, "The LORD is my portion; therefore I will wait for him."

EPHESIANS 4:31–32

Get rid of all bitterness, rage and anger, brawling and slander, along with every form of malice. Be kind and compassionate to one another, forgiving each other, just as in Christ God forgave you.

A LETTER TO *Heaven*

Dear Faithful Teacher,

Today I had the humiliating experience of being wrong. Someone younger and less experienced than I corrected me. My pride was destroyed, my ego was crushed, and my expertise was called into question.

At first, when the other person pointed out my error, I questioned the strength of his logic. *Surely*, I thought, *I could not be wrong about this.* But when he gave his explanation, it became obvious to me and to everyone else in the situation that he was right and I was wrong.

Because I was embarrassed, I became irritable and curt with him. As I look back on the situation now, I realize that I could have saved face by just thanking him for catching my error and complimenting him on his astute observation. Instead, I became flustered and tried to fix my blunder with a weak debate and a defensive argument.

Why is it so hard for me to receive instruction? I don't really believe that all knowledge lies within my grasp or that all wisdom is at my disposal. I am often in a position to teach other people, so why do I find it so hard to let someone else teach me?

While my pride is already so bruised, Lord, and while my feelings are so tender, counsel me in the ways of the wise. Lead me to an understanding of myself so that I will be receptive to the wisdom of others.

Your Floundering Follower

A LETTER FROM *Heaven*

Dear Floundering Follower,

When the soil has been turned up by the plow and prepared by the disk, it swallows up the seed and drinks in the rain. The fruitfulness of the field is enhanced by the preparation of the soil. So it is with your heart. Yet when you are hardened by pride, crusted over with self-promotion, and pressed down by self-preservation, the soil of your heart is resistant. Instruction rolls right off of the surface of your mind and never bears fruit.

Receptivity is a direct result of humility. You must uproot the pride you harbor in your heart by admitting to yourself that you are not yet everything that you could be or everything that you will be. There is much room for growth.

People with self-serving motives make many assumptions. They think more highly of themselves than they ought, and they deny themselves one of the greatest gifts of living with others—being taught by them.

Many people also fall into the trap of talking too much and listening too little. They are known by the noise they make rather than the wisdom they retain. It would not be so obvious that their heads were hollow except that their words echo with emptiness.

Learning from the younger, the wiser, and the more diligent is a part of a normal life cycle. If you think that you should be the exception, you will be—depriving yourself of an education derived from others.

Your Faithful Teacher

God's Word OF WISDOM

PSALM 119:18
Open my eyes that I may see wonderful things in your law.

PROVERBS 19:27
Stop listening to instruction, my son, and you will stray from the words of knowledge.

PROVERBS 19:20
Listen to advice and accept instruction, and in the end you will be wise.

PROVERBS 10:8–9
The wise in heart accept commands, but a chattering fool comes to ruin. The man of integrity walks securely, but he who takes crooked paths will be found out.

PSALM 119:21
You rebuke the arrogant, who are cursed and who stray from your commands.

PROVERBS 19:16
He who obeys instructions guards his life, but he who is contemptuous of his ways will die.

PROVERBS 21:24
The proud and arrogant man—"Mocker" is his
name; he behaves with overweening pride.

GALATIANS 6:6
Anyone who receives instruction in the
word must share all good things with
his instructor.

PROVERBS 21:4
Haughty eyes and a proud heart, the
lamp of the wicked, are sin!

PSALM 119:33–34
Teach me, O LORD, to follow your decrees;
then I will keep them to the end. Give me
understanding, and I will keep your law and
obey it with all my heart.

PROVERBS 23:12
Apply your heart to
instruction and your ears
to words of knowledge.

A LETTER TO *Heaven*

Dear Father of Diligence,

Some days I just don't feel like getting up and getting busy—in fact, most days. I awake to the sound of my alarm, and everything within me cries out to cover my head and stay in bed. I don't always feel like dealing with the daily grind.

Why does life have to be so demanding? Why does work—whether it is schoolwork, housework, or business—have to take up the better part of our lives? It seems to me that we should be able to make a living in half the time that we do. Then we would have more time for the things in life that are truly enjoyable.

I know several people who appear to give their best efforts in their jobs and in their academic pursuits every day. I can't relate to them. I don't understand how they muster the energy to stay with it. They intimidate me because I have to be in the mood to be productive, yet the mood rarely strikes me. I am more often in the frame of mind to watch television, talk on the phone, or engage in some sort of recreation.

Father, I have never thought of myself as lazy or unproductive. However, someone said something last week that made me realize that others may perceive me that way. I need a fresh perspective on how to maintain diligence.

Your Lazy Servant

A *L*ETTER FROM *Heaven*

Dear Lazy Servant,

You live in a fallen world, and fallen people cannot be left idle without becoming restless. Likewise, restless people cannot be left idle without becoming destructive to themselves and others. Those with too much time on their hands find things to do that lack integrity.

To be unemployed is to be disengaged in the business of living a productive life. The fact that everyone has a job to do is one of the greatest blessings to society. You will find that fulfilling the purpose for your existence is inexorably tied to your work.

There is something about the nature of mankind that only thrives when being productive. Work brings out the best qualities in people: creativity, loyalty, commitment, selflessness, cooperation, and the development of skills and talents.

The thing that you are lacking is diligence. Everyone knows what diligence is, but not everyone knows how to cultivate it. Diligence is dependent upon disciplining your spirit, mind, and body to acknowledge and act upon the divine economy. It requires the integrity to put your heart, not just your hand, to the task and do it with all of your might. Your self-respect and enjoyment of your work will increase until it is no longer discipline that compels you, but a sense of genuine fulfillment in having a job to do and doing it well.

You will be blessed beyond measure if you begin this training in diligence while in your youth.

Your Father of Great Works

God's Word OF WISDOM

PROVERBS 20:13
Do not love sleep or you will grow poor; stay awake and you will have food to spare.

PROVERBS 6:9–11
How long will you lie there, you sluggard? When will you get up from your sleep? A little sleep, a little slumber, a little folding of the hands to rest—and poverty will come on you like a bandit and scarcity like an armed man.

PROVERBS 10:4–5
Lazy hands make a man poor, but diligent hands bring wealth. He who gathers crops in summer is a wise son, but he who sleeps during harvest is a disgraceful son.

PROVERBS 6:6–8
Go to the ant, you sluggard; consider its ways and be wise! It has no commander, no overseer or ruler, yet it stores its provisions in summer and gathers its food at harvest.

48

PROVERBS 18:9
One who is slack in his work is brother to one who destroys.

PROVERBS 16:3
Commit to the LORD whatever you do, and your plans will succeed.

PROVERBS 15:32
He who ignores discipline despises himself, but whoever heeds correction gains understanding.

2 THESSALONIANS 3:6, 10–13
In the name of the Lord Jesus Christ, we command you, brothers, to keep away from every brother who is idle and does not live according to the teaching you received from us: "If a man will not work, he shall not eat." We hear that some among you are idle. They are not busy; they are busybodies. Such people we command and urge in the Lord Jesus Christ to settle down and earn the bread they eat. And as for you, brothers, never tire of doing what is right.

PROVERBS 19:15
Laziness brings on deep sleep, and the shiftless man goes hungry.

A LETTER TO *Heaven*

Dear Father of All Good Gifts,

There is a person in my life who is very needy, both emotionally and financially. She intimidates me because I know that she needs my friendship and my support. The fact is, I don't desire to give her either.

Father, am I supposed to feel responsible for hurting people just because they have placed themselves in my path? Must I become uncomfortable in order to relieve the discomfort of the less fortunate?

It is a threatening thing to be involved with someone whose needs seem to have no limits. What if she becomes dependent upon me in a way that I cannot afford? What if her emotional demands are greater than my ability to respond? I don't like the thought of being associated with her because I'm afraid she will begin to think that I'm ultimately responsible for her well-being.

Besides, Lord, I give money to many charitable causes that help the poor; that way my contribution is anonymous and safe. People benefit from my generosity without my having to get personally involved. I prefer the safety of that method to the risk of getting involved. There are plenty of people in my life with whom I can be a comrade without all that baggage. Those friendships are unintimidating and unencumbered.

But I want to do what pleases You, Lord. What do You have to say to me?

Your Struggling Servant

A LETTER FROM *Heaven*

Dear Struggling Servant,

There is a law that governs heaven and earth and makes provisions for all who live there—it is the law of love. This law has been set into motion by the God of love. It has but one dictate: Give according to the needs of people—and do so generously.

Every possessor of love's good gifts is compelled by compassion to share with those he or she finds in need of any good thing. It is that simple. However, that does not imply giving everything that is asked at every whim or on every impulse. It means responding responsibly to legitimate needs out of an abundant heart.

Long ago, I determined that among men all things would not be equal; otherwise, there would be no opportunity for people to give of themselves for the sake of others. There would be no demand of love. How could you become who I want you to be without the demands of love? You must realize that you are never more like Me than when you love enough to give of yourself.

The greatest blessings of your life will come when you give of yourself to others. Be generous with your possessions—with your time, your energy, your abilities, your privacy, and your money—and invest yourself in loving the way that you have been loved. What you gain in giving will far surpass what you keep by withholding.

Your Father of All Good Gifts

God's Word OF WISDOM

PROVERBS 22:9
A generous man will himself be blessed, for he shares his food with the poor.

PROVERBS 19:17
He who is kind to the poor lends to the LORD, and he will reward him for what he has done.

PROVERBS 14:21
He who despises his neighbor sins, but blessed is he who is kind to the needy.

1 JOHN 3:17–20
If anyone has material possessions and sees his brother in need but has no pity on him, how can the love of God be in him? Dear children, let us not love with words or tongue but with actions and in truth. This then is how we know that we belong to the truth, and how we set our hearts at rest in his presence whenever our hearts condemn us. For God is greater than our hearts, and he knows everything.

PROVERBS 3:27–28
Do not withhold good from those who deserve it, when it is in your power to act. Do not say to your neighbor, "Come back later; I'll give it tomorrow"—when you now have it with you.

PROVERBS 14:31
He who oppresses the poor shows contempt for their
Maker, but whoever is kind to the needy honors God.

PROVERBS 11:16–17
A kindhearted woman gains respect, but ruthless
men gain only wealth. A kind man benefits himself,
but a cruel man brings trouble on himself.

PROVERBS 11:24–25
One man gives freely, yet gains even
more; another withholds unduly, but
comes to poverty. A generous man
will prosper; he who refreshes others
will himself be refreshed.

MATTHEW 25:37–40
Then the righteous will answer him, "Lord,
when did we see you hungry and feed you, or
thirsty and give you something to drink?
When did we see you a stranger and invite you
in, or needing clothes and clothe you? When
did we see you sick or in prison and go to visit
you?" The King will reply, "I tell you the truth,
whatever you did for one of the least of these
brothers of mine, you did for me."

A $\mathscr{L}$ETTER TO $\mathscr{H}$eaven

Dear Father of Blessing,

I have a confession to make. I just got off the phone with a friend, and I feel despicable. I told her something about another person that I shouldn't have. At the time, I derived a feeling of great importance from the conversation. It made me feel powerful to be telling a mutual friend something that she didn't know—something that she *shouldn't* know—about another person.

The truth is, I was trying to make myself look better by disparaging that person. I don't want to be outdone by her. I'm not always happy with myself, and I get a strange sense of satisfaction from tearing someone else down when he or she appears to be out-performing me.

Lord, I know that it was wrong of me to damage her reputation. She would be so hurt if she knew, and quite honestly, I'm afraid that she will find out. I know that I would be hurt and angry if she did something like that to me. I didn't want to hurt her, and I don't want to lose her friendship; I just wanted to look good.

Lord, how do I deal with this temptation to tell things about people that I shouldn't?

I want to bless the lives of others. I want to build people up, not tear them down. I know that I don't honor You when I dishonor those whom You love.

Your Unfaithful Friend

A *Letter* from *Heaven*

Dear Friend of the Faithful One,

I am so glad that you have confessed your failure. I was aware of the conversation, of course. I can handle knowing the worst about you because I believe the best in you. I can help you to grow in this grace of blessing.

Betrayal is like a cancer. It begins as a dark shadow of selfish thought within your heart, and unless it is dealt with, it grows until it becomes a black hole that is capable of consuming the lives and reputations of those whom you love and those who love you.

Betrayal feeds off of the need to exalt yourself by tarnishing the reputations of others. It is usually riddled with untruths and slanted by hidden motives to destroy. It has a dangerous appeal and tastes so sweet upon the tongue. However, once the words have fallen upon the ears of the hearer, it becomes bitter within the heart and destroys all kinds of relationships.

Betrayal eats away at your own heart as well. Your capacity for tenderness and compassion will decay when poisoned by words that do harm to other people. The precious qualities of mercy and grace wither and die within the heart of one with an undisciplined tongue.

Put a guard upon your heart, My child, and keep from speaking words that betray others. You will be blessed by your determination to protect them from your temptation to talk.

Your Faithful Father

God's Word OF WISDOM

PROVERBS 10:12
Hatred stirs up dissension, but love covers over all wrongs.

PROVERBS 18:24
A man of many companions may come to ruin, but there is a friend who sticks closer than a brother.

PROVERBS 10:11
The mouth of the righteous is a fountain of life, but violence overwhelms the mouth of the wicked.

PROVERBS 17:27–28
A man of knowledge uses words with restraint, and a man of understanding is even-tempered. Even a fool is thought wise if he keeps silent, and discerning if he holds his tongue.

PSALM 55:12–14
If an enemy were insulting me, I could endure it; if a foe were raising himself against me, I could hide from him. But it is you, a man like myself, my companion, my close friend, with whom I once enjoyed sweet fellowship as we walked with the throng at the house of God.

PROVERBS 10:6

Blessings crown the head of the righteous, but
violence overwhelms the mouth of the wicked.

PROVERBS 10:18–19

He who conceals his hatred has lying lips, and whoever
spreads slander is a fool. When words are many, sin is not
absent, but he who holds his tongue is wise.

1 JOHN 4:20–21

If anyone says, "I love God," yet
hates his brother, he is a liar.
For anyone who does not love
his brother, whom he has seen,
cannot love God, whom he has
not seen. And he has given us
this command: Whoever loves
God must also love his brother.

GALATIANS 5:13–15

You, my brothers, were called to be free. But do
not use your freedom to indulge the sinful
nature; rather, serve one another in love. The
entire law is summed up in a single command:
"Love your neighbor as yourself." If you keep
on biting and devouring each other, watch out
or you will be destroyed by each other.

A Letter to Heaven

Dear God of Abundance,

I have never thought of myself as a materialistic person. In fact, I have always preferred a simple, uncomplicated lifestyle. But the strangest thing has happened in my heart recently, and I need Your counsel.

Lately, I have been restless and discontent. I have worked so hard all these years and have been diligent to give generously and save modestly for the future. But as I look around I feel like I've missed out. What do I have to show for all that I have invested? My friends have larger homes, more expensive cars, and better clothes. The television advertises a glamorous lifestyle that has eluded me and left me feeling empty and impoverished.

I know Your Word says that wealth isn't a source of true happiness or peace, but why is it that those who have so much seem so fulfilled? I feel that I have somehow failed. I do not measure up in comparison to those who have accumulated many material posses-sions. I had thought that my heart would be content with the unencumbered life I've chosen, but instead it seems barren and empty.

Lord, please help me understand what true riches are. I want to believe that I live in Your abundance, but I don't feel very wealthy right now. I want my values to reflect Your values. I want the joy of true worth to give meaning to my life and to spread contentment to the lives of others.

Your Unsatisfied Child

A LETTER FROM *Heaven*

Dear Unsatisfied Child,

You are tempted to place your security in the possession of many things and to indulge in the sensationalism of many thrills. Your affections are tugged by many artificial attractions. Your world places value on what can be owned and on fulfilling the immediate urge for pleasure. All of this makes contentment very elusive.

The key to abundant living is a matter of perspective. Your way of *seeing* determines whether you *feel* fulfilled.

The things that are of the greatest value are eternal things—people, relationships, integrity, and truth. You can count on this: The things you can hold in your heart, rather than in your hand, are the only true treasures. And the way you live is of far greater importance than the things you possess.

I have placed a value on you that surpasses anything that the world has to offer. You know this is true because I was willing to let My only Son leave heaven in order to keep you safe from harm. It was a great and costly sacrifice, but you are worth so much to Me. I wouldn't have done that for all the possessions or all the power in the universe. But for you, I would do anything. And I did. I did it for love.

When considering your values and measuring success, you need to consider that the only things worthy of your pursuit are things that are worthy of Me.

Your Father of Great Abundance

God's Word OF WISDOM

MATTHEW 6:19-21

Do not store up for yourselves treasures on earth, where moth and rust destroy, and where thieves break in and steal. But store up for yourselves treasures in heaven, where moth and rust do not destroy, and where thieves do not break in and steal. For where your treasure is, there your heart will be also.

PSALM 37:25-26

I was young and now I am old, yet I have never seen the righteous forsaken or their children begging bread. They are always generous and lend freely; their children will be blessed.

1 TIMOTHY 6:6-10

Godliness with contentment is great gain. For we brought nothing into the world, and we can take nothing out of it. But if we have food and clothing, we will be content with that. People who want to get rich fall into temptation and a trap and into many foolish and harmful desires that plunge men into ruin and destruction. For the love of money is a root of all kinds of evil. Some people, eager for money, have wandered from the faith and pierced themselves with many griefs.

PHILIPPIANS 4:11–13

I have learned to be content whatever the circumstances. I know what it is to be in need, and I know what it is to have plenty. I have learned the secret of being content in any and every situation, whether well fed or hungry, whether living in plenty or in want. I can do everything through him who gives me strength.

PSALM 112:1–5

Blessed is the man who fears the LORD, who finds great delight in his commands. His children will be mighty in the land; the generation of the upright will be blessed. Wealth and riches are in his house, and his righteousness endures forever. Even in darkness light dawns for the upright, for the gracious and compassionate and righteous man. Good will come to him who is generous and lends freely, who conducts his affairs with justice.

1 TIMOTHY 6:17–19

Command those who are rich in this present world not to be arrogant nor to put their hope in wealth, which is so uncertain, but to put their hope in God, who richly provides us with everything for our enjoyment. Command them to do good, to be rich in good deeds, and to be generous and willing to share. In this way they will lay up treasure for themselves as a firm foundation for the coming age, so that they may take hold of the life that is truly life.

A LETTER TO *Heaven*

Dear Tender-hearted Father,

I was in the airport today with a significant amount of time on my hands. I grew tired of reading, so I put my book aside and began to notice the looks on people's faces as they walked by. I think I observed every imaginable emotion written on the countenance of those hundreds of faces. I saw excitement, fear, anger, happiness, hurt, confusion, concentration, loneliness, and boredom. You name it, I saw it. I was amazed!

An interesting thing occurred to me as I watched. I began to realize that there are two universal truths to which I had never given much thought. One is that You have created us in such a way that we cannot keep from letting our feelings show to some degree upon our faces. The disposition reflected by our appearance states volumes about our internal condition. We are telling everyone who sees us something about our hearts.

The other interesting thing is that You have given us an amazing ability to discern these things in others. Our eyes truly are the windows to our souls. Look long enough and deep enough, and you'll see right to the core of a person.

Lord, there must be a reason that we are both so discernible and so discerning. I feel compelled to take responsibility for both what I say with my countenance and what I do in response to what I see in the faces of others.

Your Observant Follower

A LETTER FROM *Heaven*

Dear Observant Follower,

I can see that the seeds of wisdom are taking root in your heart. You are right to suspect that these two truths were intentional. There would be no expression of love if the workings of the emotional heart were as well concealed as the mechanics of the physical heart. One needs a stethoscope to discern the beat of the physical heart. One needs only a common pair of eyes to discern what beats deep within the heart of another.

Reading people can be much like reading a book, except that with people you can often judge the content by its cover.

With people, as with books, you are reading the legible lines on their faces—the up- or downturned mouth, the raised or furrowed brow, the set of the jaw. Also with people, as with books, you read between the lines. The subtle language of many micromovements are discernible only with proper interest and intuition—the twitch of an eye, the sadness behind the smile, the emptiness behind the expression.

I gave you the ability to discern these many indicators of the heart so that you would respond to them with your own. When you see sorrow on the face of another, your heart reaches to relieve it. If it were not obvious, you would never do anything about it.

From both dimensions, your vulnerability and your discernment, you are helping Me to accomplish My will among men—to love.

Your Tender-Hearted Father

God's Word OF WISDOM

GALATIANS 6:2
Carry each other's burdens,
and in this way you will fulfill
the law of Christ.

PSALM 119:66
Teach me knowledge and good judgment,
for I believe in your commands.

PROVERBS 14:30
A heart at peace gives life to the body, but
envy rots the bones.

PROVERBS 14:14
The faithless will be fully
repaid for their ways, and
the good man rewarded
for his.

PROVERBS 14:33
Wisdom reposes in the heart of the
discerning and even among fools she
lets herself be known.

PROVERBS 14:13
Even in laughter the heart may ache,
and joy may end in grief.

PROVERBS 17:24
A discerning man keeps
wisdom in view, but a
fool's eyes wander to the
ends of the earth.

PROVERBS 16:21
The wise in heart are called discerning, and pleasant
words promote instruction.

PROVERBS 16:16
How much better to get wisdom
than gold, to choose understanding
rather than silver!

1 KINGS 3:11–12
God said to him, "Since you have asked for this
and not for long life or wealth for yourself, nor
have asked for the death of your enemies but for
discernment in administering justice, I will do
what you have asked. I will give you a wise and
discerning heart, so that there will never have
been anyone like you, nor will there ever be."

A Letter to *Heaven*

Dear Lord of the Heart,

I'm frustrated today over things I cannot control or change. My hair is too curly, my teeth are not straight, I have freckles all over my face, and I'm putting on weight. In short, Lord, my appearance simply doesn't suit me.

I look around in airports, in the office, and in shopping malls and see people who seem to have all the right parts in the right proportions and in the right shape. Their complexions are clear, their muscles are toned, and they look like professional models.

Father, I know that the outward appearance is not the most important thing in life, but being attractive does seem to work to one's advantage in this culture. Whether we like it or not, there is something to be said for how we look on the outside.

Lord, teach me how to combat my feelings of futility because of my imperfect appearance. Help me find an anchor in my soul that will not shift when I'm having a bad hair day. I realize that I do not pick my friends based upon these external issues, so why do I let them dictate my acceptance of myself?

Father, I want to cherish the things that really matter because I know that I value most highly the people who understand those values.

Your Vain Child

A *Letter* from *Heaven*

Dear Vain Child,

How like you to place so much importance upon the things you see with your eyes rather than the things you perceive with your heart. I understand your appreciation of beauty because, after all, it was My idea. However, I never intended that physical beauty be more highly valued than the beauty of a pure heart, a life of integrity, or a joyful spirit.

When you consider what you are drawn to in others, you discover that you admire most the qualities of trust, compassion, authenticity, and humility. In short, you look for depth of character in others rather than perfection of appearance.

The only way to obtain true peace regarding your outward appearance is to focus on your heart. You need to direct your energies toward developing your character. The only way to do that is to take your eyes off of yourself and concentrate on the needs and concerns of others. The truly beautiful people are those whose lives are invested in the well-being of others.

True wisdom frees you from being consumed with yourself. True wisdom is a life that lavishes love, joy, kindness, and mercy upon everyone with whom it comes in contact.

Just for today, try looking past the outward appearance of people. Look into their eyes, their hearts, their souls' greatest needs, and extend yourself to touch them there. I can assure you, they will consider you the most beautiful person they have ever seen.

Your Father of Great Insight

God's Word OF WISDOM

1 SAMUEL 16:7
The LORD said to Samuel, "Do not consider his appearance or his height, for I have rejected him. The LORD does not look at the things man looks at. Man looks at the outward appearance, but the LORD looks at the heart."

PROVERBS 11:22
Like a gold ring in a pig's snout is a beautiful woman who shows no discretion.

LUKE 10:41–42
"Martha, Martha," the Lord answered, "you are worried and upset about many things, but only one thing is needed. Mary has chosen what is better, and it will not be taken away from her."

MATTHEW 6:25
I tell you, do not worry about your life, what you will eat or drink; or about your body, what you will wear. Is not life more important than food, and the body more important than clothes?

PROVERBS 12:4
A wife of noble character is her
husband's crown, but a disgraceful
wife is like decay in his bones.

1 TIMOTHY 2:9–10
I also want women to dress modestly, with decency and
propriety, not with braided hair or gold or pearls or
expensive clothes, but with good deeds, appropriate for
women who profess to worship God.

COLOSSIANS 3:12
As God's chosen people, holy and
dearly loved, clothe yourselves with
compassion, kindness, humility,
gentleness and patience.

1 PETER 3:3–4
Your beauty should not come from outward
adornment, such as braided hair and the wearing
of gold jewelry and fine clothes. Instead, it should
be that of your inner self, the unfading beauty of a
gentle and quiet spirit, which is of great worth in
God's sight.

A Letter to *Heaven*

Dear Father of Mercy,

My three sons and I saw a destitute-looking man sitting in a wheelchair today. He was begging for money just outside a major-league baseball stadium. I suppose he was there because he knew there would be thousands of people passing by. I avoided his eyes and intended to ignore him, but the boys stopped right beside his chair as the oldest called to me, "Hey, wait up."

I turned back, and there they stood, all three of them, looking at me inquisitively. Lord, I felt a hot rush of shame flood my face as I glanced into the eyes of my sons. I detected a look of disappointment in them as they realized that I was going to walk right by him. Sensing that I had intended to look past his need, they felt compelled to call me to compassion. And it wasn't until then that I noticed the man was missing both of his legs from just above the knee.

Then, Lord, I saw the look of joy on their faces as they emptied my wallet and their pockets into the man's trembling hands. His weary eyes filled with tears, and his lip quivered as he beamed at them from where he sat.

Lord, I was so ashamed of my hard heart. I want to have the eyes of a child again. I want to be spontaneously responsive to the needs of people who are less fortunate than I. I want to be sensitive and merciful to the burdened and weak. Teach me, Father, the tenderness and mercy that You have instilled within the hearts of children.

Your Hardened Follower

A LETTER FROM *Heaven*

Dear Hardened Follower,

It pleased Me to hear your thoughts on the issue of mercy. I have been putting people in your path lately who need your attention, and at last, you have responded.

I assure you, most people do what you intended to do—avoid the pain in other people's lives. The routine matters of daily living have crowded your mind with concerns that cloud your vision of others. You are so caught up in what you are doing for yourself and for your family that you forget to extend your heart to others in need.

The key to a merciful heart is humility. Children are better at responding to the needs of others because their ability to feel is more highly developed than their ability to reason. They look at people with unguarded concern. They see what you have trained your eyes to overlook. They are uninhibited about having their hearts engaged.

You still have a great capacity for genuine concern. You simply need to unleash it and let it live. Instead, you reason with yourself and harness your compassion. You talk yourself into cautious prudence instead of the unrestrained impulse to love.

Today when you see someone who needs your mercy, don't be guarded with your heart, but rather be lavish with your love. Ask yourself, "What would my children do in this situation?" The reckless abandon with which they love will not fail you.

Your Father of Reckless Love

God's Word OF WISDOM

1 PETER 1:22
Now that you have purified yourselves by obeying the truth so that you have sincere love for your brothers, love one another deeply, from the heart.

LUKE 10:25–28
On one occasion an expert in the law stood up to test Jesus. "Teacher," he asked, "what must I do to inherit eternal life?" "What is written in the Law?" he replied. "How do you read it?" He answered: "'Love the Lord your God with all your heart and with all your soul and with all your strength and with all your mind'; and, 'Love your neighbor as yourself.'" "You have answered correctly," Jesus replied. "Do this and you will live."

PHILIPPIANS 2:3–4
Do nothing out of selfish ambition or vain conceit, but in humility consider others better than yourselves. Each of you should look not only to your own interests, but also to the interests of others.

ROMANS 12:10–13

Be devoted to one another in brotherly love. Honor one another above yourselves. Never be lacking in zeal, but keep your spiritual fervor, serving the Lord. Be joyful in hope, patient in affliction, faithful in prayer. Share with God's people who are in need. Practice hospitality.

1 PETER 4:8–10

Above all, love each other deeply, because love covers over a multitude of sins. Offer hospitality to one another without grumbling. Each one should use whatever gift he has received to serve others, faithfully administering God's grace in its various forms.

JOHN 13:34

A new command I give you: Love one another. As I have loved you, so you must love one another. By this all men will know that you are my disciples, if you love one another.

ROMANS 12:9, 14–16

Love must be sincere. Hate what it evil; cling to what is good. Bless those who persecute you; bless and do not curse. Rejoice with those who rejoice; mourn with those who mourn. Live in harmony with one another. Do not be proud, but be willing to associate with people of low position. Do not be conceited.

A LETTER TO *Heaven*

Dear Father of Love,

Loving other people is a lot harder than I ever realized. If love were just a feeling, life would be so simple. I would just fall in and out of love, doing only what I felt like doing and nothing more. But as it is, I can't get by with such a simplistic approach. Love is very demanding.

It is the long haul that gets so tough, Lord. At first, I can *feel* loving toward just about anyone. I gather first impressions, usually when people are putting their best foot forward, and enjoy the thrill of discovering and being discovered.

However, by and by, those first impressions fade into reality, and the best foot is eventually overstepped by the other. Disappointment and disillusionment set in, and with them disaffection. That is when I want to pull out, Lord. It would be so much easier that way. I could say, "Hey, it was fun while it lasted. See ya!"

But that isn't your way, is it, Lord? You believe in committed love. You believe in staying when staying gets really hard. You believe in seeing it through—feeling or no feeling. And if You didn't, I would be in a heap of trouble, wouldn't I, Lord?

Father, I need some good, practical advice about how to keep my heart from abandoning the unlovable people in my life. Lead me, Father, to wisdom I can't seem to find on my own. Help me learn how to love others even when I don't feel like it.

Your Searching Child

A *Letter* from *Heaven*

Dear Searching Child,

If love were based solely upon feeling, I would have given up on you long ago—back when your heart was stone cold and your faith was nonexistent. However, I knew that your heart and your faith could be quickened by love's tender regard. I knew that My love could inspire you to become the person I intended you to be from the beginning.

When a person to whom you are struggling to stay committed seems less than he should be, you'll need to love him not because he is lovable but because it is within you to do so. You'll find you have to dig deep, reach further than you have had to go, and embrace a perspective about who he can become rather than who he is. Genuine love is so irresistibly compelling, so motivating, that you will find him rising above his mediocrity and reaching a potential that he didn't even know he had.

Committed love is sacrificial in its very essence. You are committed not to fulfilling yourself but to fulfilling the other person. And though that means you'll have to put your own needs aside in order to tend to another's, you'll find the rewards of that kind of love are unfathomably great. No greater purpose can ever be attained than to love someone enough to forget about yourself.

Join Me in this calling, My child, and you'll become just like the One who loved you so much He gave His life away so that you might live.

Your Loving Father

God's Word OF WISDOM

JOHN 15:12–13
My command is this: Love each other as I have loved you. Greater love has no one than this, that he lay down his life for his friends.

1 PETER 4:8
Above all, love each other deeply, because love covers over a multitude of sins.

JOHN 15:17
This is my command: Love each other.

1 CORINTHIANS 13:4–8
Love is patient, love is kind. It does not envy, it does not boast, it is not proud. It is not rude, it is not self-seeking, it is not easily angered, it keeps no record of wrongs. Love does not delight in evil but rejoices with the truth. It always protects, always trusts, always hopes, always perseveres. Love never fails.

EPHESIANS 5:1–2
Be imitators of God, therefore, as dearly loved children and live a life of love, just as Christ loved us and gave himself up for us as a fragrant offering and sacrifice to God.

76

PSALM 139:23–24
Search me, O God, and know
my heart; test me and know my
anxious thoughts. See if there is
any offensive way in me, and
lead me in the way everlasting.

JOHN 13:34–35
A new command I give you: Love one another.
As I have loved you, so you must love one
another. By this all men will know that you
are my disciples, if you love one another.

1 JOHN 3:23
And this is his command: to
believe in the name of his Son,
Jesus Christ, and to love one
another as he commanded us.

ACTS 2:44–47
All the believers were together and had everything
in common. Selling their possessions and goods,
they gave to anyone as he had need. Every day
they continued to meet together in the temple
courts. They broke bread in their homes and ate
together with glad and sincere hearts, praising
God and enjoying the favor of all the people.

A Letter to *Heaven*

Dear Father of Rest,

I feel like my life is out of control these days. I am so busy all of the time, yet it seems I'm getting very little accomplished. I feel harried and distracted because the demands are so pressing. In fact, I can't remember the last time I had a day off. I'm talking about a real day off—the kind when I can do anything I want to do or even do nothing at all.

My schedule is packed full, and I feel stressed all of the time. I don't know if it is because I have taken on too many obligations or if it is just poor time management. Whatever the case, I don't like the feeling that I meet myself coming and going.

I am concerned about the effect this kind of living will have on my health. I'm not sick often, but I don't sleep well and my muscles feel strained and tense all the time. I ache more than I think I should and can't identify a reason, other than stress.

I have noticed that the pressure has taken a real toll on my relationships as well. I don't have enough time for the people who really matter. I know people who have no significant relationships in their lives—no friends, no family. I have observed that they got that way by being too obligated to work, hobbies, or other pursuits. I don't want to be that way, Lord. People are the only eternal thing on this planet, and I don't want to end up alone and empty.

Lord, what should I do?

Your Weary Child

A LETTER FROM *Heaven*

Dear Weary Child,

I've been waiting for you to come to Me about this. You've piled things on your schedule until you are nearly crushed under a heap of obligations. Some of them are essential, but many are simply choices made impulsively.

There is a simple remedy for your dilemma: You need rest.

You may think that sounds *over*simplified, but it is true. You need rest. Not the kind of rest in which you just drop into bed at night at the edge of exhaustion and wake up to a screaming alarm—scrambling to make the next meeting or the next deadline. I'm not talking about recreation either. That can be as stressful as work.

The kind of rest I'm talking about is a rest you absorb in your spirit, mind, heart, and body by stepping out of your rat race and coming to a complete stop—a cessation of activity over an extended period of time. It is quiet, contemplative, restorative, and healing. That is the rest you need.

Furthermore, you need this kind of rest on a regular basis.

I know your response will be, "I can't do that; things will begin to fall apart." However, you are not as indispensable as you think you are, and the truth is that things will begin to fall apart if you *don't* rest—really rest. Stop completely and recuperate from life's demands. You'll find it will remedy your feelings of weariness and relieve your stress.

Your Father of Rest

God's Word OF WISDOM

ISAIAH 58:13–14

"If you keep your feet from breaking the Sabbath and from doing as you please on my holy day, if you call the Sabbath a delight and the LORD's holy day honorable, and if you honor it by not going your own way and not doing as you please or speaking idle words, then you will find your joy in the LORD, and I will cause you to ride on the heights of the land and to feast on the inheritance of your father Jacob." The mouth of the LORD has spoken.

MATTHEW 11:28–30

Come to me, all you who are weary and burdened, and I will give you rest. Take my yoke upon you and learn from me, for I am gentle and humble in heart, and you will find rest for your souls. For my yoke is easy and my burden is light.

PSALM 23

The LORD is my shepherd, I shall not be in want. He makes me lie down in green pastures, he leads me beside quiet waters, he restores my soul. He guides me in paths of righteousness for his name's sake. Even though I walk through the valley of the shadow of death, I will fear no evil, for you are with me; your rod and your staff, they comfort me. You prepare a table before me in the presence of my enemies. You anoint my head with oil; my cup overflows. Surely goodness and love will follow me all the days of my life, and I will dwell in the house of the LORD forever.

GENESIS 2:1–3

Thus the heavens and the earth were completed in all their vast array. By the seventh day God had finished the work he had been doing; so on the seventh day he rested from all his work. And God blessed the seventh day and made it holy, because on it he rested from all the work of creating that he had done.

ISAIAH 40:28–31

Do you not know? Have you not heard? The LORD is the everlasting God, the Creator of the ends of the earth. He will not grow tired or weary, and his understanding no one can fathom. He gives strength to the weary and increases the power of the weak. Even youths grow tired and weary, and young men stumble and fall; but those who hope in the LORD will renew their strength. They will soar on wings like eagles; they will run and not grow weary, they will walk and not be faint.

HEBREWS 4:1, 9–10

Since the promise of entering his rest still stands, let us be careful that none of you be found to have fallen short of it. There remains, then, a Sabbath-rest for the people of God; for anyone who enters God's rest also rests from his own work, just as God did from his.

EXODUS 20:8–11

Remember the Sabbath day by keeping it holy. Six days you shall labor and do all your work, but the seventh day is a Sabbath to the LORD your God. On it you shall not do any work, neither you, nor your son or daughter, nor your manservant or maidservant, nor your animals, nor the alien within your gates. For in six days the LORD made the heavens and the earth, the sea, and all that is in them, but he rested on the seventh day. Therefore the LORD blessed the Sabbath day and made it holy.

A Letter to *Heaven*

Dear Word of Life,

My mouth gets me in all kinds of trouble. It seems like I'm always saying the wrong thing at the wrong time.

I've hurt someone's feelings with my words again. I was thoughtless and rude. Honestly, I didn't intend to hurt her; I was just trying to prove my point. I wanted to win. At the time, my winning seemed more important than her feelings, but now that the damage is done, I know her feelings should have come first.

Lord, I find myself in this situation frequently. At home I get impatient when I am inconvenienced, and I say things that hurt the ones I love. My words aren't the kind that inflict deep wounds, but they are insensitive and heartless. I'm afraid that through the years they might add up to do serious harm to the relationships that mean the most to me.

I also have this problem at work. When one of my colleagues disagrees with my opinion or offers some kind of criticism, I respond curtly and make cutting remarks. I feel threatened when someone has a better idea or when my ideas are criticized.

Lord, I don't want to be unwise in my choice of words. I want to bless others by the things I say. I want my speech to be full of grace. You were always comforting people, encouraging people, loving people, healing people, delighting people, and teaching people with Your words. Can You train me, Lord, to be like You in the wisdom of Your words?

Your Outspoken Follower

A LETTER FROM *Heaven*

Dear Outspoken Follower,

Your struggle with words is so common. Everyone stumbles in what they say from time to time. But it is very important for you to realize that what you say is a direct reflection of what is in your heart. The key to using wisdom in communication begins with purifying your heart.

Think about it. The times you have disappointed yourself are the times your motives have been self-centered. Your impatience with those you love and your competitive tendency toward those with whom you work reflect a self-seeking heart rather than a heart of grace.

Perhaps that should tell you that you speak too quickly in defense of yourself and on behalf of your own desires. Maybe you should stop and consider your words before they come out of your mouth. Search your heart before you say anything, and evaluate whether your words are the right ones.

Remember, you speak harmful words when you are trying to promote your own will instead of My will. Your words should be a source of strength, hope, joy, and life to those around you. But the only way this can happen is if your heart is saturated with the wisdom of truth and grace.

My precious child, if you want to grow in wisdom, condition your heart by praying much, listening more, and saying less. You'll find that people will hunger to hear from you when you say less but say what really matters.

Your Father of Wisdom

God's Word OF WISDOM

PROVERBS 10:13
Wisdom is found on the lips of the discerning, but a rod is for the back of him who lacks judgment.

PROVERBS 10:20
The tongue of the righteous is choice silver, but the heart of the wicked is of little value.

JAMES 3:9–12
With the tongue we praise our Lord and Father, and with it we curse men, who have been made in God's likeness. Out of the same mouth come praise and cursing. My brothers, this should not be. Can both fresh water and salt water flow from the same spring? My brothers, can a fig tree bear olives, or a grapevine bear figs? Neither can a salt spring produce fresh water.

PROVERBS 10:11
The mouth of the righteous is a fountain of life, but violence overwhelms the mouth of the wicked.

84

PROVERBS 10:21
The lips of the righteous nourish many, but fools die for lack of judgment.

PROVERBS 10:19
When words are many, sin is not absent, but he who holds his tongue is wise.

PROVERBS 10:23
A fool finds pleasure in evil conduct, but a man of understanding delights in wisdom.

JAMES 3:5–8
The tongue is a small part of the body, but it makes great boasts. Consider what a great forest is set on fire by a small spark. The tongue also is a fire, a world of evil among the parts of the body. It corrupts the whole person, sets the whole course of his life on fire, and is itself set on fire by hell. All kinds of animals, birds, reptiles and creatures of the sea are being tamed and have been tamed by man, but no man can tame the tongue. It is a restless evil, full of deadly poison.

If you enjoyed this book, you'll also enjoy…

**Heavenly Mail:
Words of Love from God**
ISBN: *1-58229-234-5*

**Heavenly Mail:
Words of Promise from God**
ISBN: *1-58229-168-3*

**Heavenly Mail:
Words of Encouragement from God**
ISBN: *1-58229-169-1*

Someone you know needs a hug today...

Hugs for Grandma
ISBN: *1-58229-154-3*

Hugs for New Moms
ISBN: *1-58229-223-X*

Hugs for Girlfriends
ISBN: *1-58229-224-8*

Other great Hugs™ books

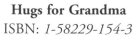

Hugs for Teens
ISBN: *1-58229-213-2*

Hugs for Daughters
ISBN: *1-58229-214-0*

Hugs for Grads
ISBN: *1-58229-155-1*

Hugs for Friends
ISBN: *1-58229-006-7*

Hugs for Sisters
ISBN: *1-58229-095-4*

Hugs for Women
ISBN: *1-878990-81-0*

Hugs for Those in Love
ISBN: *1-58229-097-0*

Hugs for Mom
ISBN: *1-878990-69-1*

Hugs for Dad
ISBN: *1-878990-70-5*

Hugs for Teachers
ISBN: *1-58229-007-5*

Hugs for the Holidays
ISBN: *1-878990-74-8*

Hugs for Grandparents
ISBN: *1-878990-80-2*

Hugs for Kids
ISBN: *1-58229-096-2*

Hugs for the Hurting
ISBN: *1-878990-68-3*

**Hugs to Encourage
and Inspire**
ISBN: *1-878990-67-5*

**Hugs from Heaven—
Celebrating Friendship**
ISBN: *1-58229-130-6*

**Hugs from Heaven—
The Christmas Story**
ISBN: *1-58229-082-2*

**Hugs from Heaven—
On Angel Wings**
ISBN: *1-878990-90-X*

**Hugs from Heaven—
Embraced by the Savior**
ISBN: *1-878990-91-8*

**Hugs from Heaven—
Portraits of a
Woman's Faith**
ISBN: *1-58229-129-2*

...it may even be you!

Heartlifters® books to make the heart soar…

Heart-shaped, foldout pages reveal personalized paraphrased Scripture

Heartlifters for Women
ISBN: *1-58229-073-3*

Other great Heartlifters® books

Heartlifters for Teachers
ISBN: *1-58229-158-6*

Heartlifters for Sisters
ISBN: *1-58229-203-5*

Heartlifters for the Hurting
ISBN: *1-58229-202-7*

Heartlifters for Sisters
ISBN: *1-58229-203-5*

**Heartlifters for
the Young at Heart**
ISBN: *1-58229-157-8*

Heartlifters for Friends
ISBN: *1-58229-100-4*

Heartlifters for Hope and Joy
ISBN: *1-58229-074-1*

Heartlifters for Mom
ISBN: *1-58229-101-2*